Created By
Angel Hepburn

Images created with the assistance of AI

Outline:

The story begins with fluffy clouds against a blue sky. One cloud gathers moisture and transforms it into a raindrop.

The raindrop starts its descent from the cloud, surrounded by other raindrops. They fall gracefully, showcasing the beauty of rain.

The raindrop lands in a puddle, creating ripples. It joins other raindrops, forming small streams that flow together.

The raindrop joins a larger river, navigating through rocks and around playful animals. The river scene is vibrant and filled with life.

The river merges with the vast ocean. The raindrop joins a mesmerizing underwater world, swimming alongside colorful fish and exploring coral reefs.

The sun's warmth causes the raindrop to evaporate, transforming into a water vapor. The scene depicts the raindrop rising as mist, lifting from the ocean's surface.

The water vapor rises higher into the atmosphere, condensing to form fluffy clouds. The raindrop becomes part of a new cloud formation.

Dark clouds gather, signaling an approaching thunderstorm. Lightning crackles across the sky, and rain begins to fall once again.

The raindrop joins other raindrops falling to the ground, nourishing plants and replenishing lakes and rivers.

The raindrop finds its way back to a puddle, completing its cyclical journey. The sky clears, and the sun shines, representing a new beginning.

www.ingramcontent.com/pod-product-compliance
Lightning Source LLC
Chambersburg PA
CBHW042251100526
44587CB00002B/98